Fugitive Pieces

George Gordon Noel Byron

Contents

BIBLIOGRAPHICAL NOTE 7
ON LEAVING N--ST--D. 11
TO E----. 13
TO D. ---- 15
TO ---- 16
TO CAROLINE. 17
TO MARIA ----. 20
TO MARY. 27
TO ---- 31
TO MARY, ON RECEIVING HER PICTURE 39
TO A LADY, ... 42
TO A BEAUTIFUL QUAKER. 44
TO JULIA! 46
TO WOMAN. 48
TO MISS E.P. 51
THE TEAR. 53
TO THE SIGHING STREPHON. 65
TO A. ---- 71

FUGITIVE PIECES

BY

George Gordon Noel Byron

TO

THOSE FRIENDS,

AT

WHOSE REQUEST THEY WERE PRINTED,

FOR WHOSE

AMUSEMENT OR APPROBATION

THEY ARE

SOLELY INTENDED;

These TRIFLES are respectfully dedicated,

BY THE

AUTHOR.

BIBLIOGRAPHICAL NOTE

Fugitive Pieces, Byron's first volume of verse, was privately printed in the autumn of 1806, when Byron was eighteen years of age. Passages in Byron's correspondence indicate that as early as August of that year some of the poems were in the printers' hands and that during the latter part of August and during September the printing was suspended in order that Byron might give his poems an "entire new form." The new form consisted, in part, in an enlargement; for he wrote to Elizabeth Pigot about September that he had nearly doubled his poems "partly by the discovery of some I conceived to be lost, and partly by some new productions." According to Moore, ***Fugitive Pieces*** was ready for distribution in November. The last poem in the volume bears the date of November 16, 1806.

A difficulty in supposing the date of completion of the volume to be about November 16 is that two copies contain inscriptions in Byron's hand with earlier dates. On the copy of the late Mr. J.A. Spoor, of Chicago, the inscription reads: "October 21st Tuesday 1806--Haec poemata ex dono sunt--Georgii Gordon Byron, Vale." That on the copy in the Morgan library reads: "Nov. 8, 1806, H.P.E.D.S.G.G.B., Southwell.--Vale!--Byron," the initials evidently standing for the Latin words of the preceding inscription. The Latin "Vale" in each inscription, however, suggests that it commemorates a leave-taking, the date referring not to the presentation but to the farewell.

It has been suggested that copies of the volume were distributed earlier than November and that some of the poems, printed separately and distributed in fly-leaf form, were added later. This would explain such discrepancies as the early dates of the inscriptions, and the presence of Byron's name on pages 46 and 48 in a volume otherwise anonymous, but there is little evidence to support it.

Moore's account of *Fugitive Pieces* is that it was distributed in November, Byron presenting the first copy to the Reverend J.T. Becher, prebendary of Southwell minster, who objected to what he considered the too voluptuous coloring of the poem "To Mary." The objection led Byron to suppress the edition immediately, he himself burning nearly every copy. This account is corroborated in part by Miss Pigot and in part by Byron.

Immediately after the destruction, Byron began the preparation of a second volume, to replace *Fugitive Pieces*. This appeared in January, 1807, as *Poems on Various Occasions*, Byron describing it as "vastly correct and miraculously chaste." Of the 38 poems that constitute Fugitive Pieces, all except "To Mary," "To Caroline," and the last six stanzas of "To Miss E.P." were reprinted in *Poems on Various Occasions*. Nineteen of the original 38 poems occur in Byron's third work, *Hours of Idleness*, published in June or July, 1807. All three editions were printed by S. and J. Ridge, booksellers of Newark, England.

Byron himself never reprinted the poems "To Mary" or "To Caroline," or the last six stanzas of "To Miss E.P." Except in a limited facsimile of *Fugitive Pieces*, supervised by H. Buxton Forman in 1886, "To Mary" has never been reprinted--not even in supposedly complete editions of Byron's works.

Only four copies of *Fugitive Pieces* are known to-day, and one of

these is incomplete. The copy from which the present facsimile is made
was originally given by Byron to Becher and preserved by him in spite
of his objections to the poem "To Mary." From Becher's family it
passed into the possession of Mr. Faulkner, of Louth, solicitor for
the Becher family. In 1885 it was in the possession of H.W. Ball,
antiquary and bookseller of Barton-on-Humber, who sold it to H. Buxton
Forman. Forman used it for his facsimile, but incorporated certain
manuscript corrections of the original, so that his facsimile is not
exact. The original is now owned by Mr. Thomas J. Wise, who has kindly
permitted its use for the present facsimile.

Of the other three copies, the incomplete one, lacking pages 17-20
("To Mary") and all after page 58, is in the possession of the family
of the late Mr. H.C. Roe, of Nottingham. This was originally sent by
Byron to Pigot, then studying medicine in Edinburgh. Byron later asked
Pigot to destroy the copy and Pigot seems to have complied so far
as to tear out the offending verses "To Mary." For many years it was
thought that only the Pigot and Becher copies had escaped destruction
at Byron's hands. But another complete copy came to light in 1907
and is now in the Pierpont Morgan Library in New York. This contains
numerous manuscript corrections and alterations, and seems to have
been used as a proof copy for **Poems on Various Occasions** (not, as
has sometimes been stated, for **Hours of Idleness**). A fourth copy,
also complete, was offered at public sale in 1912, and is now in the
hands of the executors of the late Mr. J.A. Spoor, of Chicago.

The text has been collated with that in the Morgan library, and
except for later corrections made in ink in the Morgan copy, the only
differences noted are as follows:

1.) On p. 5, in the first line of the footnote, the Morgan
copy reads "piece" where the Wise copy reads "p*ece," the
"[dotless i]" lacking.

2.) The two pages of signature M are incorrectly numbered in the Wise copy as "41, 41," this copy having no page numbered 42; and are incorrectly numbered in the Morgan copy as "40, 42," the latter copy having no page numbered 41. The text of these pages is identical.

M.K.

As these POEMS are never intended to meet the public eye, no apology is necessary for the form in which they now appear. They are printed merely for the perusal of a few friends to whom they are dedicated; who will look upon them with indulgence; and as most of them were, composed between the age of 15 and 17, their defects will be pardoned or forgotten, in the youth and inexperience of the WRITER.

ON LEAVING N--ST--D.

Through the cracks in these battlements loud the winds whistle,
  For the hall of my fathers is gone to decay;
And in yon once gay garden the hemlock and thistle
  Have choak'd up the rose, which late bloom'd in the way.

Of the barons of old, who once proudly to battle
  Led their vassals from Europe to Palestine's plain;
The escutcheon and shield, which with ev'ry blast rattle,
  Are the only sad vestiges now that remain.

No more does old Robert, with harp-stringing numbers,
  Raise a flame in the breast, for the war laurell'd wreath,
Near Askalon's Towers John of Horiston[1] slumbers,
  Unnerv'd is the hand of his minstrel by death.

Paul and Hubert too sleep in the valley of Cressy,
  For the safety of Edward and ENGLAND they fell,
My fathers! the tears of your country redress ye,
  How you fought! how you died! still her annals can tell.

On [2]Marston with Rupert[3] 'gainst traitors contending,
  Four Brothers enrich'd with their blood the bleak field
For Charles the Martyr their country defending,
  Till death their attachment to royalty scal'd.

Shades of heroes farewell! your descendant departing,
  From the seat of his ancestors, bids ye adieu!
Abroad, or at home, your remembrance imparting
  New courage, he'll think upon glory, and you.

Though a tear dims his eye at this sad separation,
  'Tis nature, not fear, which commands his regret;
Far distant he goes with the same emulation,
  In the grave, he alone can his fathers forget.

Your fame, and your memory, still will he cherish,
  He vows that he ne'er will disgrace your renown;
Like you will he live, or like you will he perish,
  When decay'd, may he mingle his dust with your own.

1803.

[1: Horiston Castle, in **Derbyshire**, an ancient seat of the B--r--n family.]

[2: The battle of **Marston Moor**, where the adherents of CHARLES I. were defeated.]

[3: Son of the Elector Palatine, and related to CHARLES I. He afterwards commanded the Fleet, in the Reign of CHARLES II.]

TO E----.

Let Folly smile, to view the names
  Of thee and me in friendship twin'd,
Yet virtue will have greater claims
  To love, than rank with vice combin'd.

And though unequal is *thy* fate,
  Since title deck'd my higher birth;
Yet envy not this gaudy state,
  Thine is the pride of modest worth.

Our *souls* at least congenial meet,
  Nor can *thy* lot *my* rank disgrace;
Our intercourse is not less sweet,
  Since worth of rank supplies the place.

November, 1802.

ON THE DEATH OF A YOUNG LADY, COUSIN TO THE AUTHOR AND VERY DEAR TO HIM.

    Hush'd are the winds, and still the evening gloom,
      Not e'en a zephyr wanders through the grove,
    Whilst I return to view my Margaret's tomb,
      And scatter flowers on the dust I love.

2.

    Within this narrow cell reclines her clay,
      That clay where once such animation beam'd;
    The king of terrors seiz'd her as his prey,
      Not worth, nor beauty, have her life redeem'd.

3.

    Oh! could that king of terrors pity feel,
      Or Heaven reverse the dread decree of fate,
    Not here the mourner would his grief reveal,
      Not here the muse her virtues would relate.

4.

    But wherefore weep! her matchless spirit soars,
      Beyond where aplendid shines the orb of day.
    And weeping angels lead her to those bowers,
      Where endless pleasures virtuous deeds repay.

5.

And shall presumptuous mortals Heaven arraign!
  And madly God-like Providence accuse!
Ah! no far fly from me attempts so vain,
  I'll ne'er submission to my God refuse.

6.

Yet is remembrance of those virtues dear,
  Yet fresh the memory of that beauteous face;
Still they call forth my warm affection's tear.
  Such sorrow brings me honour, not disgrace.[4]

1802.

[4: The Author claims the indulgence of the reader, more for this piece, than, perhaps, any other in the collection; but as it was written at an earlier period than the rest, (being composed at the age of 14) and his first Essay, be preferred submitting it to the indulgence of his friends in its present state, to making either addition or alteration.]

TO D. ----

In thee, I fondly hop'd to clasp,
  A friend whom death alone could sever,
But envy with malignant grasp,
  Has torn thee from my breast for ever.

2.

   True, she has forc'd thee from my *breast*,
     But in my *heart* thou keep'st thy seat;
   There, there, thine image still must rest,
     Until that heart shall cease to beat.

3.

   And when the grave restores her dead,
     When life again to dust is given,
   On *thy dear* breast I'll lay my head,
     Without *thee*! *where* would be *my Heaven?*

February, 1803.

TO ----

   Think'st thou I saw thy beauteous eyes,
     Suffus'd in tears implore to stay;
   And heard *unmov'd*, thy plenteous sighs,
     Which said far more than words could say.

   Though deep the grief, *thy* tears exprest,
     When love, and hope, lay *both* o'erthrown,
   Yet still, my girl, *this* bleeding breast,
     Throbb'd with deep sorrow, as *thine own*.

   But when our cheeks with anguish glow'd,
     When *thy* sweet lips where join'd to mine;
   The tears that from *my* eye-lids flow'd,

Were lost in those which fell from *thine*.

Thou could'st not feel my burning cheek,
   Thy gushing tears had quench'd its flame,
And as thy tongue essay'd to speak,
   In *sighs alone* it breath'd my name.

And yet, my girl, we weep in vain,
   In vain our fate in sighs deplore;
Remembrance only can remain,
   But *that*, will make us weep the more.

Again, thou best belov'd, adieu!
   Ah! if thou canst o'ercome regret,
Nor let thy mind past joys review,
   Our only *hope* is to *forget*.

1805.

TO CAROLINE.

You say you love, and yet your eye
   No symptom of that love conveys,
You say you love, yet know not why,
   Your cheek no sign of love betrays.

2.

Ah! did that breast with ardour glow,
With me alone it joy could know,
Or feel with me the listless woe,

    Which racks my heart when far from thee.

3.

    Whene'er we meet my blushes rise,
      And mantle through my purpled cheek,
    But yet no blush to mine replies,
      Nor e'en your eyes your love bespeak.

4.

    Your voice alone declares your flame,
      And though so sweet it breaths my name;
    Our passions still are not the same,
      Alas! you cannot love like me.

5.

    For e'en your lip seems steep'd in snow,
      And though so oft it meets my kiss,
    It burns with no responsive glow,
      Nor melts like mine in dewy bliss.

6.

    Ah! what are words to love like mine,
    Though uttered by a voice like thine,
    I still in murmurs must repine,
      And think that love can ne'er be true.

7.

  Which meets me with no joyous sign,
    Without a sigh which bids adieu;
  How different is my love from thine,
    How keen my grief when leaving you.

8.

  Your image fills my anxious breast,
  Till day declines adown the West,
  And when, at night, I sink to rest,
    In dreams your fancied form I view.

9.

  'Tis then your breast, no longer cold,
    With equal ardour seems to burn,
  While close your arms around me fold,
    Your lips my kiss with warmth return.

10.

  Ah! would these joyous moments last;
  Vain HOPE! the gay delusions past,
  That voice!--ah! no, 'tis but the blast,
    Which echoes through the neighbouring grove.

11.

  But when *awake*, your lips I seek,
    And clasp enraptur'd all your charms,
  So chill's the pressure of your cheek,

  I fold a statue in my arms.

12.

If thus, when to my heart embrac'd,
No pleasure in your eyes is trac'd,
You may be prudent, fair, and chaste,
 But ah! my girl, you *do not love*.

TO MARIA ----

Since now the hour is come at last,
 When you must quit your anxious lover,
Since now, our dream of bliss is past,
 One pang, my girl, and all is over.

Alas! that pang will be severe,
 Which bids us part, to meet no more;
Which tears me far from *one* so dear,
 Departing for a distant shore.

Well! we have pass'd some happy hours,
 And joy will mingle with our tears;
When thinking on these ancient towers,
 The shelter of our infant years.

Where from this gothic casement's height,
 We view'd the lake, the park, the dell,
And still though tears obstruct our sight,
 We lingering look a last farewell.--

O'er fields, through which we us'd to run,
  And spend the hours in childish play,
O'er shades where, when our race was done,
  Reposing on my breast you lay,

Whilst I, admiring, too remiss,
  Forgot to scare the hovering flies,
Yet envied every fly the kiss,
  It dar'd to give your slumbering eyes.

See still the little painted *bark*,
  In which I row'd you o'er the lake;
See there, high waving o'er the park,
  The *elm*, I clamber'd for your sake.

These times are past, our joys are gone,
  You leave me, leave this happy vale;
These scenes, I must retrace alone,
  Without thee, what will they avail.

Who can conceive, who has not prov'd,
  The anguish of a last embrace?
When torn from all you fondly lov'd,
  You bid a long adieu to peace.

This is the deepest of our woes,
  For *this*, these tears our cheeks bedew,
This is of love the final close,
  Oh GOD! the fondest, *last* adieu!

1805.

FRAGMENTS OF SCHOOL EXERCISES, FROM THE PROMETHEUS VINCTUS OF AESCHYLUS.

Great Jove! to whose Almighty Throne,
  Both Gods and mortals homage pay,
Ne'er may my soul thy power disown,
  Thy dread behests ne'er disobey.
Oft shall the sacred victim fall,
In sea-girt Ocean's mossy hall;
My voice shall raise no impious strain,
'Gainst him who rules the sky and azure main.

How different now thy joyless fate,
  Since first Hesione thy bride,
When plac'd aloft in godlike state,
  The blushing beauty by thy side.
Thou sat'st, while reverend Ocean smil'd,
And mirthful strains the hours beguil'd;
The nymphs and Tritons danc'd around,
Nor yet thy doom was fix'd nor Jove relentless frown'd.

HARROW, *December* 1, 1804.

LINES IN "LETTERS OF AN ITALIAN NUN AND AN ENGLISH GENTLEMAN," BY J.J. ROUSSEAU, FOUNDED ON FACTS.

Away, away,--your flattering arts,
May now betray some simpler hearts;
And *you* will *smile* at their believing,
And *they* shall *weep* at your deceiving.

ANSWER TO THE ABOVE, ADDRESS'D TO MISS ----.

Dear simple girl those flattering arts,
(From which you'd guard frail female hearts,)
Exist but in imagination,
Mere phantoms of your own creation;
For he who sees that witching grace,
That perfect form, that lovely face;
With eyes admiring, oh! believe me,
He never wishes to deceive thee;
Once let you at your mirror glance,
You'll there descry that elegance,
Which from our sex demands such praises,
But envy in the other raises.--
Then he who tells you of your beauty,
Believe me only does his duty;
Ah! fly not from the candid youth,
It is not flattery, but truth.

July, 1804.

ON A CHANGE OF MASTERS, AT A GREAT PUBLIC SCHOOL.

Where are those honours? IDA, once your own,
When Probus fill'd your magisterial throne;
As ancient Rome fast falling to disgrace,
Hail'd a Barbarian in her Caesar's place;
So you degenerate share as hard a fate,
And seat **Pomposus**, where your **Probus** sate.
Of narrow brain, but of a narrower soul,
Pomposus, holds you in his harsh controul;
Pomposus, by no social virtue sway'd,
With florid jargon, and with vain parade;
With noisy nonsense, and new fangled rules,
(Such as were ne'er before beheld in schools,)
Mistaking *pedantry*, for *learning's* laws,
He governs, sanctioned but by self applause.
With him, the same dire fate attending Rome,
Ill-fated IDA! soon must stamp your doom;
Like her o'erthrown, forever lost to fame,
No trace of science left you, but the name.

HARROW, *July*, 1805.

EPITAPH ON A BELOVED FRIEND.

Oh Boy! forever lov'd, for ever dear,
What fruitless tears have wash'd thy honour'd bier;
What sighs re-echoed to thy parting breath,
Whilst thou wert struggling in the pangs of death.
Could tears have turn'd the tyrant in his course,
Could sighs have check'd his dart's relentless force;
Could youth and virtue claim a short delay,
Or beauty charm the spectre from his prey.
Thou still had'st liv'd, to bless my aching sight,
Thy comrade's honour, and thy friend's delight:
Though low thy lot, since in a cottage born,
No titles did thy humble name adorn,
To me, far dearer, was thy artless love,
Than all the joys, wealth, fame, and friends could prove.
For thee alone I liv'd, or wish'd to live,
(Oh God! if impious, this rash word forgive)
Heart broken now, I wait an equal doom,
Content to join thee in thy turf-clad tomb;
Where this frail form compos'd in endless rest,
I'll make my last, cold, pillow on thy breast;
That breast where oft in life, I've laid my head,
Will yet receive me mouldering with the dead;
This life resign'd without one parting sigh,
Together in one bed of earth we'll lie!
Together share the fate to mortals given,
Together mix our dust, and hope for Heaven.

HARROW, 1803.

ADRIAN'S ADDRESS TO HIS SOUL, WHEN DYING.

   Animula! vagula, Blandula,
   Hospes, comesque, corporis,
   Quoe nunc abibis in Loca?
   Pallidula, rigida, nudula,
   Nec ut soles dabis Jocos.

TRANSLATION.

  Ah! gentle, fleeting, wav'ring sprite!
  Friend and associate of this clay,
    To what unknown region borne,
  Wilt thou now wing thy distant flight?
  No more with wonted humour gay,
    But pallid, cheerless, and forlorn.

1806.

TO MARY.

Rack'd by the flames of jealous rage,
  By all her torments deeply curst,
  Of hell-born passions far the worst,
What hope my pangs can now assuage?

2.

I tore me from thy circling arms,
  To madness fir'd by doubts and fears,
  Heedless of thy suspicious tears,
Nor feeling for thy feign'd alarms.

3.

Resigning every thought of bliss,
  Forever, from your love I go,
  Reckless of all the tears that flow,
Disdaining thy polluted kiss.

4.

No more that bosom heaves for me,
  On it another seeks repose,
  Another riot's on its snows,
Our bonds are broken, both are free.

5.

   No more with mutual love we burn,
     No more the genial couch we bless,
     Dissolving in the fond caress;
   Our love o'erthrown will ne'er return.

6.

   Though love than ours could ne'er be truer,
     Yet flames too fierce themselves destroy,
     Embraces oft repeated cloy,
   Ours came too *frequent*, to endure.

7.

   You quickly sought a second lover,
     And I too proud to share a heart,
     Where once I held the *whole*, not *part*,
   Another mistress must discover.

8.

   Though not the *first* one, who hast blest me,
     Yet I will own, you was the dearest,
     The one, unto my bosom nearest;
   So I conceiv'd, when I possest thee.

9.

   Even now I cannot well forget thee,
     And though no more in folds of pleasure,
     Kiss follows kiss in countless measure,

I hope *you* sometimes will regret me.

10.

And smile to think how oft were done,
  What prudes declare a sin to act is,
  And never but in darkness practice,
Fearing to trust the tell-tale sun.

11.

And wisely therefore night prefer,
  Whose dusky mantle veils their fears,
  Of *this*, and *that*, of eyes and ears,
Affording shades to those that err.

12.

Now, by my foul, 'tis most delight
  To view each other panting, dying.
  In love's *extatic posture* lying,
Grateful to *feeling*, as to *sight*.

13.

And had the glaring God of Day,
  (As formerly of Mars and Venus)
  Divulg'd the joys which pass'd between us,
Regardless of his *peeping* ray.

14.

Of love admiring such a ***sample***,
  The Gods and Goddesses descending,
  Had never fancied us offending,
But ***wisely*** followed ***our example***.

When to their airy hall, my father's voice,
Shall call my spirit, joyful in their choice,
When pois'd upon the gale, my form shall ride,
Or dark in mist, descend the mountain's side;
Oh! may my shade behold no sculptur'd urns,
To mark the spot, where earth to earth returns.
No lengthen'd scroll of virtue, and renown,
My ***epitaph***, shall be my name alone;
If ***that*** with honour fails to crown my clay,
Oh! may no other fame my deeds repay;
That, only ***that***, shall single out the shot,
By ***that*** remember'd, or fore'er forgot.--

1803.

TO ----

1.

Oh! when shall the grave hide forever my sorrow?
   Oh! when shall my soul wing her flight from this clay?
The present is hell! and the coming to-morrow,
   But brings with new torture, the curse of to-day.

2.

From my eye flows no tear, from my lips fall no curses,
   I blast not the fiends, who have hurl'd me from bliss,
For poor is the soul which bewailing rehearses,
   Its querulous grief, when in anguish like this--

3.

Was my eye, 'stead of tears, with red fury flakes bright'ning.
   Would my lips breathe a flame, which no stream could assuage,
On our foes should my glance launch in vengeance its lightning,
   With transport my tongue give a loose to its rage.

4.

But now tears and curses alike unavailing,
   Would add to the souls of our tyrants delight;
Could they view us, our sad separation bewailing,
   Their merciless hearts would rejoice at the sight.

5.

Yet still though we bend with a feign'd resignation,
  Life beams not for us with one ray that can cheer,
Love and hope upon earth bring no more consolation,
  In the grave is our hope, for in life is our fear.

6.

Oh! when, my ador'd, in the tomb will they place me,
  Since in life, love and friendship, for ever are fled,
If again in the mansion of death I embrace thee,
  Perhaps they will leave unmolested--the dead.

1805.

1.

When I hear you express an affection so warm,
  Ne'er think, my belov'd, that I do not believe,
For your lip, would the soul of suspicion disarm,
  And your eye beams a ray, which can never deceive.

2.

Yet still, this fond bosom regrets whilst adoring,
  That love like the leaf, must fall into the sear,
That age will come on, when remembrance deploring,
  Contemplates the scenes of her youth, with a tear.

3.

That the time must arrive, when no longer retaining
  Their auburn, these locks must wave thin to the breeze.
When a few silver hairs of those tresses remaining,
  Prove nature a prey to decay, and disease.

4.

'Tis this, my belov'd, which spreads gloom o'er my features
  Tho' I ne'er shall presume to arraign the decree;
Which God has proclaim'd as the fate of his creatures,
  In the death which one day will deprive me of thee.

5.

No jargon of priests o'er our union was mutter'd,
  To rivet the fetters of husband and wife;
By our lips, by our hearts, were our vows alone utter'd,
  To perform them, in full, would ask more than a life.

6.

But as death my belov'd, soon or late, shall o'ertake us,
  And our breasts which alive with such sympathy glow,
Will sleep in the grave, till the blast shall awake us,
  When calling the dead, in earth's bosom laid low.

7.

Oh! then let us drain, while we may, draughts of pleasure,
  Which from passion like ours will unceasingly flow;
Let us pass round the cup of love's bliss in full measure,

And quaff the contents as our nectar below.

1805.

ON A DISTANT VIEW OF THE VILLAGE AND SCHOOL OF HARROW ON THE HILL.
1806.

Ye scenes of my childhood, whose lov'd recollection,
  Embitters the present, compar'd with the past;
Where science first dawn'd on the powers of reflection,
  And friendships were form'd, too romantic to last.

2.

Where fancy yet joys, to retrace the resemblance,
  Of comrades in friendship, and mischief allied;
How welcome once more your ne'er fading remembrance,
  Which rests in the bosom, though hope is deny'd.

3.

Again I revisit the hills where we sported,
  The streams where we swam, and the fields where we fought;
The school where loud warn'd by the bell we resorted,
  To pore o'er the precepts by Pedagogues taught.

4.

Again I behold where for hours I have ponder'd,
  As reclining at eve on yon tombstone I lay;
Or round the steep brow of the churchyard I wander'd,
  To catch the last gleam of the sun's setting ray.

5.

I once more view the room with spectators surrounded,
  Where as Zanga I trod on Alonzo o'erthrown;
While to swell my young pride such applauses resounded,
  I fancied that MOSSOP[5] himself was outshone.

6.

Or as Lear I pour'd for the deep imprecation,
  By my daughters of kingdom and reason depriv'd:
Till fir'd by loud plaudits, and self adulation,
  I consider'd myself as a **Garrick** reviv'd.

7.

Ye dreams of my boyhood how much I regret you,
  As your memory beams through this agoniz'd breast,
Thus sad and deserted, I ne'er can forget you,
  Though this heart throbs to bursting by anguish possest.

8.

I thought this poor brain fever'd even to madness,
  Of tears as of reason forever was drain'd,
But the drops which now flow down *this* bosom of sadness,

    Convince me, the springs have some moisture retain'd.

9.

    Sweet scenes of my childhood! your blest recollection,
      Has wrung from these eye-lids to weeping long dead,
    In torrents, the tears of my warmest affection,
      The last and the fondest, I ever shall shed.

[5: MOSSOP, a cotempory of GARRICK, famous for his performance of *Zanga*, in YOUNG's tragedy of the *Revenge*.]

THOUGHTS SUGGESTED BY A COLLEGE EXAMINATION.

High in the midst surrounded by his peers,
M--ns--l his ample front sublime uprears;
Plac'd on his chair of state, he seems a God,
While Sophs and Freshmen, tremble at his nod.
Whilst all around sit wrapt in speechless gloom,
His voice in thunder shakes the sounding dome;
Denouncing dire reproach, to luckless fools,
Unskill'd to plod in mathematic rules.

Happy the youth! in Euclid's axioms tried,
Though little vers'd in any art beside;
Who with scarce sense to pen an *English* letter,
Yet with precision, scans an *attic metre*.

What! though he knows not how his fathers bled,
When civil discord pil'd the fields with dead,
When Edward bade his conquering bands advance,
Or Henry trampled on the crest of France;
Though marvelling at the name of *Magna Charta*,
Yet, well he recollects the *laws of Sparta*.
Can tell what edicts sage *Lycurgus* made,
Whilst *Blackstone's* on the *shelf neglected* laid;
Of *Grecian dramas* vaunts the deathless fame,
Of *Avon's bard*, remembering scarce the name.

Such is the youth, whose scientific pate,
Class honours, medals, fellowships await;
Or even perhaps the *declamation* prize,
If to such glorious height, he lifts his eyes.
But lo! no *common* orator can hope
The envied silver cup within his scope;
Not that our *heads* much eloquence require,
The ATHENIAN's glowing style, or TULLY's fire.
The *manner* of the speech is nothing, since
We do not try by *speaking* to *convince*;
Be other *orators* of pleasing *proud*,
We speak to *please* ourselves, not *move* the crowd.
Our gravity prefers the *muttering* tone,
A proper mixture of the *squeak and groan*;
No borrow'd *grace* of *action*, must be seen,
The slightest motion would displease the *dean*.
Whilst every staring graduate would prate,
Against what, *he* could never imitate.

The man, who hopes t' obtain the promis'd cup,
Must in one *posture* stand, and *ne'er look up*,

Nor *stop*, but rattle over *every* word,
No matter *what*, so it can *not* be heard;
Thus let him hurry on, nor think to rest,
Who speaks the *fastest*, 's sure to speak the *best*;
Who utters most within the shortest space,
May safely hope to win the *wordy race*.

The sons of *Science these*, who thus repaid,
Linger in ease, in Granta's sluggish shade;
Where on Cam's sedgy banks supine they lie,
Unknown, unhonour'd live, unwept for, die.
Dull as the pictures, which adorn their halls,
They think all learning fix'd within their walls:
In manners rude, in foolish forms precise,
All modern arts, affecting to despise.
Yet prizing Bentley's[6] Brunck's[6] or *Porson's*[7] note,
More than the *verse, on which the critic wrote*;
With eager haste, they court the tool of power,
(Whether 'tis PITT or PETTY rules the hour:)
To *him*, with suppliant smiles they bend the head,
Whilst mitres, prebends, to their eyes are spread.
But should a storm o'erwhelm him with disgrace,
They'd fly to seek the next, who fill'd his place;
Such are the men who learning's treasures guard,
Such is their *practice*, such is their *reward*;
This *much* at least we may presume to say,
Th' *reward's* scarce equal, to the *price* they *pay*.

1806.

[6: Celebrated Critics.]

[7: The present Greek Professor at Cambridge.]

TO MARY, ON RECEIVING HER PICTURE.

1.

This faint resemblance of thy charms,
  (Though strong as mortal art could give)
My constant heart of fear disarms,
  Revives my hopes, and bids me live.

2.

Here I can trace the locks of gold,
  Which round thy snowy forehead wave,
The cheeks which sprung from Beauty's mould,
  The lips which made me *Beauty's* slave.

3.

Here I can trace--ah no! that eye,
  Whose azure floats in liquid fire,
Must all the painter's art defy,
  And bid him from the task retire.

4.

Here I behold, its beauteous hue,
  But where's the beam of soft desire?
Which gave a lustre to its blue,

Love, only love, could e'er inspire.

5.

Sweet copy! far more dear to me,
  Lifeless, unfeeling as thou art,
Than all the living forms could be,
  Save her, who plac'd thee next my heart.

6.

She plac'd it, sad with needless fear,
  Lest time might shake my wavering soul,
Unconscious that her image there,
  Held every sense in fast controul.

7.

Through hours, through years, through time 'twill cheer,
  My hope in gloomy moments raise;
In life's last conflict 't'will appear,
  And meet my fond, expiring gaze.

ON THE DEATH OF MR. FOX, THE FOLLOWING ILLIBERAL IMPROMPTU APPEARED IN THE MORNING POST.

"Our Nation's foes, lament on *Fox's* death,
"But bless the hour, when PITT resign'd his breath;
"These feelings wide, let Sense and Truth unclue,
"We give the palm, where Justice points its due."

To which the Author of these Pieces, sent the subjoined Reply, for Insertion in the MORNING CHRONICLE.--

Oh! factious viper! whose envenom'd tooth,
Would mangle still the dead, in spite of truth,
What though our "nation's foes" lament the fate,
With generous feeling, of the good and great;
Shall therefore dastard tongues assail the name
Of him whose virtues claim eternal fame?
When PITT expired in plenitude of power,
Though ill success obscur'd his dying hour,
Pity her dewy wings before him spread,
For noble spirits "war not with the dead;"
His friends in tears, a last sad requiem gave,
And all his errors slumber'd in the grave.
He died an Atlas, bending 'neath the weight,
Of cares oppressing our unhappy state;
But lo! another Hercules appear'd,
Who for a time, the ruined fabric rear'd;
He too is dead! who still our England propp'd,

With him our fast reviving hopes have dropp'd;
Not one great people only raise his urn,
All Europe's far extended regions mourn.
"These feelings wide, let Sense and Truth unclue,
"And give the palm where Justice points it due;"
But let not canker'd calumny assail,
And round our statesman wind her gloomy veil.
Fox! o'er whose corse a mourning world must weep,
Whose dear remains in honoured marble sleep;
For whom at last, even hostile nations groan,
And friends and foes alike his talents own;
Fox! shall in Britain's future annals shine,
Nor e'en to ***Pitt***, the patriot's ***palm*** resign;
Which Envy, wearing Candour's sacred mask,
For PITT, and PITT alone, would dare to ask.

TO A LADY, WHO PRESENTED THE AUTHOR A LOCK OF HAIR, BRAIDED WITH HIS OWN, AND APPOINTED A NIGHT IN DECEMBER, TO MEET HIM IN THE GARDEN.

These locks which fondly thus entwine,
In firmer chains our hearts confine;
Than all th' unmeaning protestations,
Which swell with nonsense, love orations.
Our love is fix'd, I think we've prov'd it,
Nor time, nor place, nor art, have mov'd it;
Then wherefore should we sigh, and whine,

With groundless jealousy repine.
With silly whims, and fancies frantic,
Merely to make our love romantic.
Why should you weep like *Lydia Languish*,
And fret with self-created anguish.
Or doom the lover you have chosen,
On winter nights, to sigh half frozen:
In leafless shades, to sue for pardon,
Only because the scene's a garden.
For gardens seem by one consent
(Since SHAKESPEARE set the precedent;)
(Since Juliet first declar'd her passion)
To form the place of assignation.
Oh! would some modern muse inspire,
And seat her by a *sea-coal* fire,
Or had the bard at Christmas written,
And laid the scene of love in Britain;
He surely in commiseration,
Had chang'd the place of declaration.
In Italy I've no objection,
Warm nights are proper for reflection;
But here, our climate is so rigid,
That love itself, is rather frigid;
Think on our chilly situation,
And curb this rage for imitation.
Then let us meet, as oft we've done,
Beneath the influence of the sun;
Or, if at midnight I must meet you,
Oh! let me in your chamber greet you;
There we can love for hours together,
Much better in such snowy weather,
Than plac'd in all th' Arcadian groves,
That ever witness'd rural loves;

There if my passion fail to please,
Next night I'll be content to freeze;
No more I'll give a loose to laughter,
But curse my fate, forever after.

TO A BEAUTIFUL QUAKER.

Sweet girl! though only once we met,
That meeting I shall ne'er forget;
And though we ne'er may meet again,
Remembrance will thy form retain;
I would not say, "I love" but still
My senses struggle with my will;
In vain to drive thee from my breast,
My thoughts are more and more represt,
In vain, I check the rising sighs,
Another to the last replies;
Perhaps this is not love, but yet
Our meeting I can ne'er forget.

What though we never silence broke,
Our eyes a sweeter language spoke;
The tongue in flattering falsehood deals,
And tells a tale, it never feels;
Deceit, the guilty lips impart,
And hush the mandates of the heart,
But soul's interpreters, the eyes
Spurn such restraint, and scorn disguise.
As thus our glances oft convers'd,
And all our bosoms felt, rehears'd,

No *spirit* from within reprov'd us,
Say rather, "'twas the *spirit mov'd us*."
Though what they utter'd, I repress,
Yet, I conceive, thou'lt partly guess;
For, as on thee, my memory ponders,
Perchance, to me thine also wanders;
This for myself, at least I'll say,
Thy form appears through night, through day,
Awake, with it my fancy teems,
In sleep, it smiles in fleeting dreams;
The vision charms the hours away,
And bids me curse Aurora's ray;
For breaking slumbers of delight,
Which make me wish for endless night.
Since, oh! whate'er my future fate,
Shall joy or woe my steps await;
Tempted by love, by storms beset,
Thine image, I can ne'er forget.

Alas! again no more we meet,
No more our former looks repeat;
Then let me breathe this parting prayer,
The dictate of my bosom's care:
"May Heaven so guard my lovely quaker,
"That anguish never can o'ertake her;
"That peace and virtue ne'er forsake her,
"But bliss be aye, her heart's partaker:
"No jealous passion shall invade,
"No envy that pure breast pervade;"
For he that revels in such charms,
Can never seek another's arms;
"Oh! may the happy mortal fated,
"To be by dearest ties related;

"For ***her*** each hour ***new joy*** discover,
"And lose the husband in the lover.
"May that fair bosom never know
"What 'tis to feel the restless woe;
"Which stings the soul, with vain regret,
"Of him, who never can forget."

TO JULIA!

Julia! since far from you I've rang'd,
  Our souls with fond affection glow not;
You say 'tis I, ***not you*** have chang'd,
  I'd tell you why,--but yet I know not.

2.

Your polish'd brow, no cares have crost,
  And Julia! we are not much older,
Since trembling first my heart I lost,
  Or told my love with hope, grown bolder.

3.

Sixteen was then our utmost age,
  Two years have lingering pass'd away, love!
And now new thoughts our minds engage,
  At least, ***I*** feel disposed to stray, love!

4.

'Tis *I*, that am alone to blame,
  I, that am guilty of love's treason;
Since your sweet breast, is still the same,
  Caprice must be my only reason.

5.

I do not, love, suspect your truth,
  With jealous doubt my bosom heaves not,
Warm was the passion of my youth,
  One trace of dark deceit it leaves not.

6.

No, no, my flame was not pretended,
  For oh! I lov'd you most sincerely,
And though our dream at last is ended,
  My bosom still esteems you dearly.

7.

No more we meet in yonder bowers,
  Perhaps my soul's too prone to roving,
But older, firmer **hearts** than ours,
  Have found monotony in loving.

8.

Your cheeks soft bloom is unimpair'd,
  Your beauties still are daily bright'ning,
Your eye for conquest comes prepar'd,

The forge of love's resistless lightning.

9.

Arm'd thus to make their bosoms bleed,
  Many will throng to sigh like me, love,
More constant they may prove indeed,
  Fonder alas! they ne'er can be, love!

TO WOMAN.

Surely experience might have told me,
That all must love thee, who behold thee;
Surely experience might have taught,
A woman's promises are naught,
But plac'd in all thy charms before me,
All I forget, but to *adore* thee.
Oh memory! thou choicest blessing,
When join'd with hope, when still possessing;
Thou whisperest, as our hearts are beating,
"What oft we've done, we're still repeating."
But how much curst by every lover,
When hope is fled, and passion's over.
Woman that fair and fond deceiver,
How prompt are striplings to believe her,
How throbs the pulse, when first we view,
The eye that rolls in glossy blue;
Or sparkles black, or mildly throws,
A beam from under hazel brows;
How quick we credit every oath,

And hear her plight the willing troth;
Fondly we hope 'twill last for aye,
When lo! she changes in a day,
The Record will forever stand,
"That woman's vows, are writ in sand."

AN OCCASIONAL PROLOGUE DELIVERED BY THE AUTHOR, PREVIOUS TO THE PERFORMANCE OF THE WHEEL OF FORTUNE, AT A PRIVATE THEATRE.

Since the refinement of this polish'd age,
Has swept immoral raillery from the stage;
Since taste has now expung'd licentious wit,
Which stamp'd disgrace on all an author writ;
Since now to please with purer scenes we seek,
Nor dare to call the blush from beauty's cheek;
Oh! let the modest muse some pity claim,
And meet indulgence--though she find not fame.
But not for *her* alone, we wish respect,
Others appear more conscious of defect;
To night, no **Veteran Roscii** you behold,
In all the arts of scenic action old;
No COOKE, no KEMBLE, can salute you here,
No SIDDONS draw the sympathetic tear,
To night, you thong to witness the debut,
Of embryo actors to the drama new;
Here then, our almost unfledg'd wings we try,

Clip not our ***pinions***, ere the ***birds can fly***;
Failing in this our first attempt to soar,
Drooping, alas, we fall to rise no more.
Not one poor trembler only, fear betrays,
Who hopes, yet almost dreads to meet your praise;
But all our Dramatis Personae wait,
In fond suspense, this crisis of their fate;
No venal views our progress can retard,
Your generous plaudits are our sole reward;
For them each ***Hero*** all his power displays,
Each timid ***Heroine*** shrinks before your gaze:
Surely these last will some protection find,
None to the softer sex can prove unkind;
Whilst youth and beauty form the female shield,
The sternest critic to the fair must yield.
But should our feeble efforts nought avail,
Should, ***after all***, our best endeavours fail;
Still let some mercy in your bosoms live,
And if you can't applaud, at least ***forgive***.

TO MISS E.P.

1.

Eliza! what fools are the Mussulman sect,
  Who to woman deny the soul's future existence,
Could they see thee, Eliza! they'd own their defect,
  And this doctrine would meet with a general resistance.

2.

Had their Prophet possess'd but an atom of sense,
  He ne'er would have **woman** from Paradise driven,
But instead of his **Houris** a flimsy pretence,
  With **woman alone**, he had peopled his Heaven.

3.

But still to increase your calamities more,
  Not content with depriving your bodies of spirit,
He allots but **one husband** to share amongst four,
  With **souls** you'd dispense--but this last who could bear it.

4.

His religion to please neither **party** is made,
  On **husbands** 'tis **hard**, to the wives most uncivil;
But I can't contradict what so oft has been said,
  "Though women are angels, yet wedlock's the devil."

5.

This terrible truth, even Scripture has told,
  Ye Benedicks! hear me, and listen with rapture;
If a glimpse of redemption you wish to behold,
  Of St. MATT.--read the second and twentieth chapter.

6.

'Tis surely enough upon earth to be vex'd,
  With wives who eternal confusion are spreading;
"But in Heaven" (so runs the Evangelist's Text,)
  "We neither have giving in marriage, or wedding."

7.

From this we suppose, (as indeed well we may,)
  That should Saints after death, with their spouses put up more,
And wives, as in life, aim at absolute sway,
  All Heaven would ring with the conjugal uproar.

8.

Distraction and discord would follow in course,
  Nor MATTHEW, nor MARK, nor St. PAUL, can deny it,
The only expedient is general divorce,
  To prevent universal disturbance and riot.

9.

But though husband and wife, shall at length be disjoin'd
  Yet woman and man ne'er were meant to dissever,
Our chains once dissolv'd, and our hearts unconfin'd,

We'll love without bonds, but we'll love you forever.

10.

Though souls are denied you by fools and by rakes,
  Should you own it yourselves, I would even then doubt you,
Your nature so much of *celestial* partakes,
  The Garden of Eden would wither without you.

SOUTHWELL, *October* 9, 1806.

THE TEAR.

1.

When Friendship or Love,
  Our sympathies move,
When Truth in a glance should appear,
  The lips may beguile,
  With a dimple or smile,
But the test of affection's a *tear*.

2.

Too oft is a smile,
  But the hypocrite's wile,
To mask detestation, or fear,
  Give me the soft sigh,
  Whilst the soul telling eye

Is dimm'd, for a time, with a ***tear***.

3.

   Mild charity's glow,
    To us mortals below,
Shows the soul from barbarity clear,
    Compassion will melt,
    Where this virtue is felt,
And its dew is diffused in a ***tear***.

4.

   The man doom'd to sail,
    With the blast of the gale,
Through billows Atlantic to steer,
    As he bends o'er the wave,
    Which may soon be his grave,
The green sparkles bright with a ***tear***.

5.

   The soldier braves death,
    For a fanciful wreath,
In Glory's romantic career;
    But he raises the foe,
    When in battle laid low,
And bathes every wound with a ***tear***.

6.

   When with high bounding pride,
    He returns to his bride,

Renouncing the gore crimson'd spear;
  All his toils are repaid,
  When embracing the maid,
From her eyelid he kisses the tear.

7.

Sweet scene of my youth,
  Seat of Friendship and Truth,
Where Love chac'd each fast-fleeting year,
  Loth to leave thee I mourn'd,
  For a last look I turn'd,
But thy spire was scarce seen through a *tear*.

8.

Though my vows I can pour,
  To my Mary no more,
My Mary to love once so ***dear***,
  In the shade of her bower,
  I remember the hour,
She rewarded those vows with a *tear*.

9.

By another possest,
  May she live ever blest,
Her name still my heart must revere,
  With a sigh I resign,
  What I once thought was mine,
And forgive her deceit with a *tear*.

10.

 Ye friends of my heart,
 Ere from you I depart,
This hope to my breast is most near,
 If again we shall meet,
 In this rural retreat,
May we *meet*, as we *part*, with a *tear*.

11.

 When my soul wings her flight,
 To the regions of night,
And my body shall sleep on its bier;
 As ye pass by the tomb,
 Where my ashes consume,
Oh! moisten their dust with a *tear*.

12.

 May no marble bestow,
 The splendour of woe,
Which the children of Vanity rear,
 No fiction of fame,
 Shall blazon my name,
All I ask, all I wish, is a *tear*.

BYRON, *October 26*, 1806.

REPLY TO SOME VERSES OF J.M.B. PIGOT, ESQ. ON THE CRUELTY OF HIS MISTRESS.

1.

    Why PIGOT, complain,
      Of this damsel's disdain,
   Why thus in despair, do you fret?
      For months you may try,
      But believe me a *sigh*,
   Will never obtain a coquette.

2.

    Would you teach her to love,
      For a time seem to rove,
   At first she may *frown* in a *pet*;
      But leave her awhile,
      She shortly will smile,
   And then you may *kiss* your *coquette*.

3.

    For such are the airs,
      Of these fanciful fairs,
   They think all our *homage* a *debt*;
      But a partial neglect,
      Soon takes an effect,

And humbles the proudest *coquette*.

4.

   Dissemble your pain,
    And lengthen your chain,
Nor seem her *hauteur* to *regret*,
    If again you shall sigh,
    She no more will deny,
That *yours* is the rosy *coquette*.

5.

   But if from false pride,
    Your pangs she deride,
This whimsical virgin forget;
    Some *other* admire,
    Who will *melt* with your *fire*,
And laugh at the *little* coquette.

6.

   For *me*, I adore,
    Some *twenty* or more,
And love them most dearly, but yet,
    Though my heart they enthral,
    I'd abandon them all,
Did they act like your blooming *coquette*.

7.

   No longer repine,
    But form this design,

And break through her slight woven net;
  Away with despair,
  No longer forbear,
To fly from the captious coquette.

8.

  Then quit her, my friend!
  Your bosom defend,
Ere quite with her snares you're beset;
  Lest your deep wounded heart
  When incens'd by the smart,
Should lead you to *curse* the coquette.

BYRON, *October* 27, 1806.

GRANTA, A MEDLEY.

Oh! could LE SAGE's[8] demon's gift,
  Be realized at my desire,
This night my trembling form he'd lift,
  And place it on St. Mary's spire.

2.

Then would unroof'd old Granta's Halls
  Pedantic inmates full display,
Fellows who dream on *lawn*, or *stalls*,
  The price of hireling votes to pay.

3.

> Then would I view each rival Wight,
>   PETTY and PALMERSTON survey,
> Who canvass now with all their might,
>   Against the next elective day.

4.

> One on his power and place depends,
>   The other on the Lord knows what,
> Each to some eloquence pretends,
>   But neither will convince by ***that***.

5.

> The first indeed may not demur,
>   Fellows are sage reflecting men,
> And know preferment can occur,
>   But very seldom, ***now*** and ***then***.

6.

> They know the Chancellor has got,
>   Some pretty livings in disposal,
> Each hopes that ***one*** may be his ***lot***,
>   And therefore smiles at his proposal.

7.

> Now from corruption's shameless scene,
>   I'll turn mine eye, as night grows later,
> And view unheeded, and unseen,

The studious sons of Alma Mater.

8.

There in apartments small and damp,
  The candidate for college prizes,
Sits poring by the midnight lamp,
  Goes late to bed and early rises.

9.

He surely well deserves to gain them,
  And all the honours of His college,
Who striving hardly to obtain them,
  Thus seeks unprofitable knowledge.

10.

Who sacrifices hours of rest,
  To scan precisely metres attic,
And agitates his anxious breast,
  In solving problems mathematic.

11.

Who reads false quantities in Sele,[9]
  Or puzzles o'er the deep triangle,
And robs himself of many a meal,
  In ***barbarous latin***[10] doom'd to wrangle.

12.

>Renouncing every pleasing page,
>   From authors of historic use,
>Preferring to the lettered sage,
>   The square of the hypothenuse.[11]

13.

>But harmless are these occupations,
>   Which hurt none but the hapless student;
>Compared with other recreations,
>   Which bring together the imprudent.

14.

>Whose daring revels shock the sight,
>   When vice and infamy combine,
>When drunkenness and dice unite,
>   And every sense is steep'd in wine.

15.

>Not so the methodistic crew,
>   Who plans of reformation lay,
>In humble attitude they sue,
>   And for the sins of others pray.

16.

>Forgetting that their pride of spirit,
>   And exultation in their trial;
>Detracts most largely from the merit,

Of all their boasted self-denial.

17.

'Tis morn,--from these I turn my sight,
  What scene is this which meets the eye,
As numerous crowd array'd in white,[12]
  Across the green in numbers fly.

18.

Loud rings in air, the chapel bell,
  'Tis hush'd,--what sounds are these I hear,
The organ's soft celestial swell,
  Rolls deeply on the listening ear.

19.

To this is join'd the sacred song,
  The royal minstrel's hallowed strain,
But *he* who hears the *music* long,
  Will *never* wish to *hear again*.

20.

Our choir would scarcely be excus'd,
  Even as a band of raw beginners,
But mercy now must be refus'd,
  To such a set of croaking sinners.

21.

If David when his toils were ended,
  Had heard these blockheads sing before him,
To us his psalms had ne'er descended,
  In furious mood he would have tore 'em.

22.

The luckless Israelites when taken,
  By some inhuman tyrant's order,
Were ask'd to sing, by joy forsaken,
  On Babylonian river's border.

23.

But had they sung in notes like these,
  Inspir'd by stratagem, or fear,
They might have set their hearts at ease,
  The devil a soul had stay'd to hear.

24.

But if I write much longer now,
  The deuce a soul ***will stay to read***,
My pen is blunt, the ink is low,
  'Tis almost time to ***stop, indeed***.

25.

Therefore farewell, old GRANTA's spires,
  No more like ***Cleofas*** I fly,
No more thy theme my muse inspires,

The reader's tired, and so am I.

October 28, 1806.

[8: The Diable Boiteux of LE SAGE, where Asmodeus the Demon, places Don Cleofas on an elevated situation, and unroofs the houses for his inspection.]

[9: Sele's publication on Greek metres is not remarkable for its accuracy.]

[10: Every Cambridge man will assent to this,--the Latin of the Schools is almost unintelligible.]

[11: The discovery of Pythagoras, that the square of the Hypothenuse, is equal to the squares of the other two sides of a right angled triangle.]

[12: On a Saint Day, the Students wear Surplices in Chapel.]

TO THE SIGHING STREPHON.

  Your pardon my friend,
   If my rhymes did offend,
Your pardon a thousand times o'er,
   From friendship I strove,
   Your pangs to remove,
But I swear I will do so no more.

2.

   Since your ***beautiful*** maid
    Your flame has repaid,
No more I your folly regret;
   She's now most divine,
    And I bow at the shrine,
Of this quickly reformed coquette.

3.

   But still I must own,
    I should never have known,
From ***your verses*** what else she deserv'd,
   Your pain seem'd so great,
    I pitied your fate,
As your fair was so dev'lish reserv'd.

4.

   But since the chaste kiss,
    Of this magical Miss,
Such wonderful transports produce,
   Since the "world you forget,"
    "When your lips once have met,"
My Counsel will get but abuse.

5.

   You say "when I rove"
    "I know nothing of love,"
'Tis true I am given to range,
   If I rightly remember,

I've kiss'd a good number,
But there's pleasure at least in a change.

6.

   I ne'er will advance,
   By the rules of romance,
To humour a whimsical fair,
   Though a smile may delight,
   Yet a *frown* wont *affright*,
Or drive me to dreadful despair.

7.

   Whilst my blood is thus warm,
   I ne'er shall reform,
To mix in the Platonist's school;
   Of this I am sure,
   Was my passion so pure,
My mistress must think me *a fool*.

8.

   Though the kisses are sweet,
   Which voluptuously meet,
Of kissing I ne'er was so fond,
   As to make me forget,
   Though our lips oft have met,
That still there was *something beyond*.

9.

   And if I should shun,
    Every *woman* for *one*,
Whose *image* must fill my whole breast;
    Whom I must *prefer*,
    And *sigh* but for *her*,
What an *insult* 'twould be to the *rest*!

10.

   Now, Strephon, good bye,
    I cannot deny,
Your passion appears most absurd,
    Such *love* as you plead,
    Is *pure* love indeed,
For it *only* consists in the *word*.

THE CORNELIAN.

No specious splendour of this stone,
  Endears it to my memory ever,
With lustre ***only once*** it shone,
  But blushes modest as the giver.

2.

Some who can sneer at friendship's ties,
  Have for my weakness oft reprov'd me,
Yet still the simple gift I prize,
  For I am sure, the giver lov'd me.

3.

He offered it with downcast look,
  As ***fearful*** that I might refuse it,
I told him when the gift I took,
  My ***only fear*** should be to lose it.

4.

This pledge attentively I view'd,
  And ***sparkling*** as I held it near,
Methought one drop the stone bedew'd,
  And ever since ***I've lov'd a tear***.

5.

>Still to adorn his humble youth,
> Nor wealth nor birth their treasures yield,
>But he who seeks the flowers of truth,
> Must quit the garden for the field.

6.

>'Tis not the plant uprear'd in sloth,
> Which beauty shews, and sheds perfume,
>The flowers which yield the most of both,
> In nature's wild luxuriance bloom.

7.

>Had Fortune aided nature's care,
> For once forgetting to be blind,
>*His* would have been an ample share,
> If well proportioned to his mind.

8.

>But had the Goddess clearly seen,
> His form had fixed her fickle breast,
>*Her* countless hoards would *his* have been,
> And none remain'd to give the rest.

TO A. ----

Oh! did those eyes instead of fire,
  With bright, but mild affection shine,
Though they might kindle less desire,
  Love, more than mortal, would be thine.

2.

For thou art form'd so heavenly fair,
  Howe'er those orbs ***may*** wildly beam,
We ***must*** admire, but still despair,
  That fatal glance forbids esteem.

3.

When nature stamp'd thy beauteous birth,
  So much perfection in thee shone,
She fear'd, that too divine for earth,
  The skies might claim thee for their own.

4.

Therefore to guard her dearest work,
  Lest angels might dispute the prize,
She bade a secret lightning lurk,
  Within those once celestial eyes.

5.

These might the boldest Sylph appal,
  When gleaming with meridian blaze,

Thy beauty must enrapture all,
  But who can dare thine ardent gaze?

6.

'Tis said that Berenice's hair,
  In stars adorns the vault of heaven,
But they would ne'er permit *thee* there,
  Thou would'st so far outshine the seven.

7.

For did those eyes as planets roll,
  Thy sister lights would scarce appear,
E'en suns which systems now controul,
  Would twinkle dimly through their sphere.

Friday, Nov. 7th, 1806.

AS THE AUTHOR WAS DISCHARGING HIS PISTOLS IN A GARDEN, TWO LADIES PASSING NEAR THE SPOT, WERE ALARMED BY THE SOUND OF A BULLET HISSING NEAR THEM. TO ONE OF WHOM THE FOLLOWING VERSES ON THE OCCASION, WERE ADDRESSED THE NEXT MORNING.

1.

Doubtless, sweet girl, the hissing lead,
   Wafting destruction near thy charms,
And hurtling[13] o'er thy lovely head,
   Has fill'd that breast with fond alarms.

2.

Surely some envious Demon's force,
   Vex'd to behold such beauty here,
Impell'd the bullet's viewless course,
   Diverted from its first career.

3.

Yes! in that nearly fatal hour,
   The ball obey'd some hell-born guide,
But Heaven with interposing power,
   In pity turn'd the death aside.

4.

> Yet, as perchance one trembling tear,
>   Upon that thrilling bosom fell,
> Which *I*, th' unconscious cause of fear,
>   Extracted from its glistening cell;--

5.

> Say, what dire penance can atone?
>   For such an outrage done to thee,
> Arraign'd before thy beauty's throne,
>   What punishment wilt thou decree?

6.

> Might I perform the Judge's part,
>   The sentence I should scarce deplore.
> It only would restore a heart,
>   Which but belong'd to **thee** before.

7.

> The least atonement, I can make,
>   Is to become no longer free,
> Henceforth, I breathe, but for thy sake.
>   Thou shall be **all in all** to me.

8.

> But thou perhaps may'st now reject
>   Such expiation of my guilt,
> Come then--some other mode elect?

Let it be death--or what thou wilt.

9.

Choose then relentless! and I swear,
  Nought shall thy dread decree prevent,
Yet hold--one little word forbear!
  Let it be aught but **banishment**.

[13: This word is used by GRAY in his poem to the fatal Sisters:--

"Iron sleet of arrowy shower,
Hurtles through the darken'd air."

TRANSLATION FROM CATULLUS. AD LESBIAM.

Equal to Jove, that youth must be,
Greater than Jove he seems to me;
Who free from Jealousy's alarms,
Securely views thy matchless charms;
That cheek which ever dimpling glows,
That mouth from whence such music flows;
To him alike are always known,
Reserv'd for him, and him alone.
Ah Lesbia! though 'tis death to me,
I cannot choose, but look on thee;
But at the sight, my senses fly,
I needs must gaze, but gazing die;
Whilst trembling with a thousand fears,

Parch'd to the throat, my tongue adheres.
My pulse beats quick, my breath heaves short,
My limbs deny their slight support.
Cold dews my pallid face o'erspread,
With deadly languor droops my head.
My ears with tingling echoes ring,
And life itself is on the wing;
My eyes refuse the cheering light,
Their orbs are veil'd in starless night:
Such pangs my nature sinks beneath,
And feels a temporary death.--

TRANSLATION OF THE EPITAPH ON VIRGIL AND TIBULLUS, BY DOMITIUS MARSUS.

He who sublime in epic numbers roll'd,
  And he who struck the softer lyre of love,
By Death's [14]unequal hand alike controul'd,
Fit comrades in Elysian regions move.

[14: The hand of Death is said to be unjust or unequal, as Virgil was considerably older than Tibullus, at his decease.]

IMITATION OF TIBULLUS "SULPICIA AD CERINTUM." LIB. QUART.

Cruel Cerintus! does this fell disease,
Which racks my breast, your fickle bosom please.
Alas! I wish'd but to o'ercome the pain,
That I might live for love, and you again,
But now I scarcely shall bewail my fate,
By Death alone, I can avoid your hate.

TRANSLATION FROM CATULLUS. LUCTUS DE NORTE PASSERIS.

Ye Cupids droop each little head,
Nor let your wings with joy be spread,
My Lesbia's favourite bird is dead,
  Which dearer than her eyes she lov'd:
For he was gentle and so true,
Obedient to her call he flew,
No fear, no wild alarm he knew,
  But lightly o'er her bosom mov'd.

And softly fluttering here, and there,
He never sought to cleave the air,
But chirrup'd oft, and free from care,
  Tun'd to her ear his grateful strain.

But now he's pass'd the gloomy bourn,
From whence he never can return,
His death, and Lesbia's grief I mourn,
  Who sighs alas! but sighs in vain.

Oh curst be thou! devouring grave!
Whose jaws eternal victims crave,
From whom no earthly power can save,
  For thou hast ta'en the bird away.
From thee, my Lesbia's eyes o'erflow,
Her swollen cheeks with weeping glow,
Thou art the cause of all her woe,
  Receptacle of life's decay.

IMITATED FROM CATULLUS. TO ANNA.

Oh! might I kiss those eyes of fire,
A million scarce would quench desire,
Still would I steep my lips in bliss,
And dwell an age on every kiss;
Nor then my soul should sated be,
Still would I kiss, and cling to thee,
Nought should my kiss from thine dissever.
Still would we kiss, and kiss forever;
E'en though the number did exceed,
The yellow harvest's countless seed,
To part would be a vain endeavour,
Could I desist?--ah! never--never.

November 16, 1806.

www.bookjungle.com *email: sales@bookjungle.com fax: 630-214-0564 mail: Book Jungle PO Box 2226 Champaign, IL 61825*

The Codes Of Hammurabi And Moses
W. W. Davies

QTY

The discovery of the Hammurabi Code is one of the greatest achievements of archaeology, and is of paramount interest, not only to the student of the Bible, but also to all those interested in ancient history...

Religion   **ISBN:** *1-59462-338-4*   Pages:132
                                              MSRP $12.95

The Theory of Moral Sentiments
Adam Smith

QTY

This work from 1749. contains original theories of conscience amd moral judgment and it is the foundation for systemof morals.

Philosophy   **ISBN:** *1-59462-777-0*   Pages:536
                                              MSRP $19.95

Jessica's First Prayer
Hesba Stretton

QTY

In a screened and secluded corner of one of the many railway-bridges which span the streets of London there could be seen a few years ago, from five o'clock every morning until half past eight, a tidily set-out coffee-stall, consisting of a trestle and board, upon which stood two large tin cans, with a small fire of charcoal burning under each so as to keep the coffee boiling during the early hours of the morning when the work-people were thronging into the city on their way to their daily toil...

Childrens   **ISBN:** *1-59462-373-2*   Pages:84
                                              MSRP $9.95

My Life and Work
Henry Ford

QTY

Henry Ford revolutionized the world with his implementation of mass production for the Model T automobile. Gain valuable business insight into his life and work with his own auto-biography... "We have only started on our development of our country we have not as yet, with all our talk of wonderful progress, done more than scratch the surface. The progress has been wonderful enough but..."

Biographies/ **ISBN:** *1-59462-198-5*   Pages:300
                                              MSRP $21.95

www.bookjungle.com email: sales@bookjungle.com fax: 630-214-0564 mail: Book Jungle PO Box 2226 Champaign, IL 61825

The Art of Cross-Examination
Francis Wellman

QTY

I presume it is the experience of every author, after his first book is published upon an important subject, to be almost overwhelmed with a wealth of ideas and illustrations which could readily have been included in his book, and which to his own mind, at least, seem to make a second edition inevitable. Such certainly was the case with me; and when the first edition had reached its sixth impression in five months, I rejoiced to learn that it seemed to my publishers that the book had met with a sufficiently favorable reception to justify a second and considerably enlarged edition. ..

Reference   ISBN: *1-59462-647-2*   Pages:412   MSRP *$19.95*

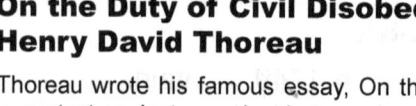

On the Duty of Civil Disobedience
Henry David Thoreau

QTY

Thoreau wrote his famous essay, On the Duty of Civil Disobedience, as a protest against an unjust but popular war and the immoral but popular institution of slave-owning. He did more than write—he declined to pay his taxes, and was hauled off to gaol in consequence. Who can say how much this refusal of his hastened the end of the war and of slavery ?

Law   ISBN: *1-59462-747-9*   Pages:48   MSRP *$7.45*

Dream Psychology Psychoanalysis for Beginners
Sigmund Freud

QTY

Sigmund Freud, born Sigismund Schlomo Freud (May 6, 1856 - September 23, 1939), was a Jewish-Austrian neurologist and psychiatrist who co-founded the psychoanalytic school of psychology. Freud is best known for his theories of the unconscious mind, especially involving the mechanism of repression; his redefinition of sexual desire as mobile and directed towards a wide variety of objects; and his therapeutic techniques, especially his understanding of transference in the therapeutic relationship and the presumed value of dreams as sources of insight into unconscious desires.

Psychology   ISBN: *1-59462-905-6*   Pages:196   MSRP *$15.45*

The Miracle of Right Thought
Orison Swett Marden

QTY

Believe with all of your heart that you will do what you were made to do. When the mind has once formed the habit of holding cheerful, happy, prosperous pictures, it will not be easy to form the opposite habit. It does not matter how improbable or how far away this realization may see, or how dark the prospects may be, if we visualize them as best we can, as vividly as possible, hold tenaciously to them and vigorously struggle to attain them, they will gradually become actualized, realized in the life. But a desire, a longing without endeavor, a yearning abandoned or held indifferently will vanish without realization.

Self Help   ISBN: *1-59462-644-8*   Pages:360   MSRP *$25.45*

www.bookjungle.com *email: sales@bookjungle.com fax: 630-214-0564 mail: Book Jungle PO Box 2226 Champaign, IL 61825*

QTY

☐ **The Rosicrucian Cosmo-Conception Mystic Christianity** *by Max Heindel*   ISBN: *1-59462-188-8* **$38.95**
The Rosicrucian Cosmo-conception is not dogmatic, neither does it appeal to any other authority than the reason of the student. It is: not controversial, but is: sent forth in the, hope that it may help to clear..
New Age/Religion Pages 646

☐ **Abandonment To Divine Providence** *by Jean-Pierre de Caussade*   ISBN: *1-59462-228-0* **$25.95**
"The Rev. Jean Pierre de Caussade was one of the most remarkable spiritual writers of the Society of Jesus in France in the 18th Century. His death took place at Toulouse in 1751. His works have gone through many editions and have been republished...
Inspirational/Religion Pages 400

☐ **Mental Chemistry** *by Charles Haanel*   ISBN: *1-59462-192-6* **$23.95**
Mental Chemistry allows the change of material conditions by combining and appropriately utilizing the power of the mind. Much like applied chemistry creates something new and unique out of careful combinations of chemicals the mastery of mental chemistry...
New Age Pages 354

☐ **The Letters of Robert Browning and Elizabeth Barret Barrett 1845-1846 vol II**   ISBN: *1-59462-193-4* **$35.95**
by Robert Browning and Elizabeth Barrett
Biographies Pages 596

☐ **Gleanings In Genesis (volume I)** *by Arthur W. Pink*   ISBN: *1-59462-130-6* **$27.45**
Appropriately has Genesis been termed "the seed plot of the Bible" for in it we have, in germ form, almost all of the great doctrines which are afterwards fully developed in the books of Scripture which follow...
Religion/Inspirational Pages 420

☐ **The Master Key** *by L. W. de Laurence*   ISBN: *1-59462-001-6* **$30.95**
In no branch of human knowledge has there been a more lively increase of the spirit of research during the past few years than in the study of Psychology, Concentration and Mental Discipline. The requests for authentic lessons in Thought Control, Mental Discipline and...
New Age/Business Pages 422

☐ **The Lesser Key Of Solomon Goetia** *by L. W. de Laurence*   ISBN: *1-59462-092-X* **$9.95**
This translation of the first book of the "Lernegton" which is now for the first time made accessible to students of Talismanic Magic was done, after careful collation and edition, from numerous Ancient Manuscripts in Hebrew, Latin, and French...
New Age/Occult Pages 92

☐ **Rubaiyat Of Omar Khayyam** *by Edward Fitzgerald*   ISBN:*1-59462-332-5* **$13.95**
Edward Fitzgerald, whom the world has already learned, in spite of his own efforts to remain within the shadow of anonymity, to look upon as one of the rarest poets of the century, was born at Bredfield, in Suffolk, on the 31st of March, 1809. He was the third son of John Purcell...
Music Pages 172

☐ **Ancient Law** *by Henry Maine*   ISBN: *1-59462-128-4* **$29.95**
The chief object of the following pages is to indicate some of the earliest ideas of mankind, as they are reflected in Ancient Law, and to point out the relation of those ideas to modern thought.
Religion/History Pages 452

☐ **Far-Away Stories** *by William J. Locke*   ISBN: *1-59462-129-2* **$19.45**
"Good wine needs no bush, but a collection of mixed vintages does. And this book is just such a collection. Some of the stories I do not want to remain buried for ever in the museum files of dead magazine-numbers an author's not unpardonable vanity..."
Fiction Pages 272

☐ **Life of David Crockett** *by David Crockett*   ISBN: *1-59462-250-7* **$27.45**
"Colonel David Crockett was one of the most remarkable men of the times in which he lived. Born in humble life, but gifted with a strong will, an indomitable courage, and unremitting perseverance...
Biographies/New Age Pages 424

☐ **Lip-Reading** *by Edward Nitchie*   ISBN: *1-59462-206-X* **$25.95**
Edward B. Nitchie, founder of the New York School for the Hard of Hearing, now the Nitchie School of Lip-Reading, Inc, wrote "LIP-READING Principles and Practice". The development and perfecting of this meritorious work on lip-reading was an undertaking...
How-to Pages 400

☐ **A Handbook of Suggestive Therapeutics, Applied Hypnotism, Psychic Science**   ISBN: *1-59462-214-0* **$24.95**
by Henry Munro
Health/New Age/Health/Self-help Pages 376

☐ **A Doll's House: and Two Other Plays** *by Henrik Ibsen*   ISBN: *1-59462-112-8* **$19.95**
Henrik Ibsen created this classic when in revolutionary 1848 Rome. Introducing some striking concepts in playwriting for the realist genre, this play has been studied the world over.
Fiction/Classics/Plays 308

☐ **The Light of Asia** *by sir Edwin Arnold*   ISBN: *1-59462-204-3* **$13.95**
In this poetic masterpiece, Edwin Arnold describes the life and teachings of Buddha. The man who was to become known as Buddha to the world was born as Prince Gautama of India but he rejected the worldly riches and abandoned the reigns of power when...
Religion/History/Biographies Pages 170

☐ **The Complete Works of Guy de Maupassant** *by Guy de Maupassant*   ISBN: *1-59462-157-8* **$16.95**
"For days and days, nights and nights, I had dreamed of that first kiss which was to consecrate our engagement, and I knew not on what spot I should put my lips..."
Fiction/Classics Pages 240

☐ **The Art of Cross-Examination** *by Francis L. Wellman*   ISBN: *1-59462-309-0* **$26.95**
Written by a renowned trial lawyer, Wellman imparts his experience and uses case studies to explain how to use psychology to extract desired information through questioning.
How-to/Science/Reference Pages 408

☐ **Answered or Unanswered?** *by Louisa Vaughan*   ISBN: *1-59462-248-5* **$10.95**
Miracles of Faith in China
Religion Pages 112

☐ **The Edinburgh Lectures on Mental Science (1909)** *by Thomas*   ISBN: *1-59462-008-3* **$11.95**
This book contains the substance of a course of lectures recently given by the writer in the Queen Street Hall, Edinburgh. Its purpose is to indicate the Natural Principles governing the relation between Mental Action and Material Conditions...
New Age/Psychology Pages 148

☐ **Ayesha** *by H. Rider Haggard*   ISBN: *1-59462-301-5* **$24.95**
Verily and indeed it is the unexpected that happens! Probably if there was one person upon the earth from whom the Editor of this, and of a certain previous history, did not expect to hear again...
Classics Pages 380

☐ **Ayala's Angel** *by Anthony Trollope*   ISBN: *1-59462-352-X* **$29.95**
The two girls were both pretty, but Lucy who was twenty-one who supposed to be simple and comparatively unattractive, whereas Ayala was credited, as her Bombwhat romantic name might show, with poetic charm and a taste for romance. Ayala when her father died was nineteen...
Fiction Pages 484

☐ **The American Commonwealth** *by James Bryce*   ISBN: *1-59462-286-8* **$34.45**
An interpretation of American democratic political theory. It examines political mechanics and society from the perspective of Scotsman James Bryce
Politics Pages 572

☐ **Stories of the Pilgrims** *by Margaret P. Pumphrey*   ISBN: *1-59462-116-0* **$17.95**
This book explores pilgrims religious oppression in England as well as their escape to Holland and eventual crossing to America on the Mayflower, and their early days in New England...
History Pages 268

www.bookjungle.com email: sales@bookjungle.com fax: 630-214-0564 mail: Book Jungle PO Box 2226 Champaign, IL 61825

			QTY
The Fasting Cure *by Sinclair Upton*	ISBN: *1-59462-222-1*	**$13.95**	☐
In the Cosmopolitan Magazine for May, 1910, and in the Contemporary Review (London) for April, 1910, I published an article dealing with my experiences in fasting. I have written a great many magazine articles, but never one which attracted so much attention... New Age/Self Help/Health Pages 164			
Hebrew Astrology *by Sepharial*	ISBN: *1-59462-308-2*	**$13.45**	☐
In these days of advanced thinking it is a matter of common observation that we have left many of the old landmarks behind and that we are now pressing forward to greater heights and to a wider horizon than that which represented the mind-content of our progenitors... Astrology Pages 144			
Thought Vibration or The Law of Attraction in the Thought World	ISBN: *1-59462-127-6*	**$12.95**	☐
by William Walker Atkinson	Psychology/Religion Pages 144		
Optimism *by Helen Keller*	ISBN: *1-59462-108-X*	**$15.95**	☐
Helen Keller was blind, deaf, and mute since 19 months old, yet famously learned how to overcome these handicaps, communicate with the world, and spread her lectures promoting optimism. An inspiring read for everyone... Biographies/Inspirational Pages 84			
Sara Crewe *by Frances Burnett*	ISBN: *1-59462-360-0*	**$9.45**	☐
In the first place, Miss Minchin lived in London. Her home was a large, dull, tall one, in a large, dull square, where all the houses were alike, and all the sparrows were alike, and where all the door-knockers made the same heavy sound... Childrens/Classic Pages 88			
The Autobiography of Benjamin Franklin *by Benjamin Franklin*	ISBN: *1-59462-135-7*	**$24.95**	☐
The Autobiography of Benjamin Franklin has probably been more extensively read than any other American historical work, and no other book of its kind has had such ups and downs of fortune. Franklin lived for many years in England, where he was agent... Biographies/History Pages 332			

Name	
Email	
Telephone	
Address	
City, State ZIP	

☐ Credit Card   ☐ Check / Money Order

Credit Card Number	
Expiration Date	
Signature	

Please Mail to: Book Jungle
PO Box 2226
Champaign, IL 61825
or Fax to: 630-214-0564

ORDERING INFORMATION

web: *www.bookjungle.com*
email: *sales@bookjungle.com*
fax: *630-214-0564*
mail: *Book Jungle PO Box 2226 Champaign, IL 61825*
or PayPal *to sales@bookjungle.com*

Please contact us for bulk discounts

DIRECT-ORDER TERMS

**20% Discount if You Order
Two or More Books**
Free Domestic Shipping!
Accepted: Master Card, Visa,
Discover, American Express

www.ingramcontent.com/pod-product-compliance
Lightning Source LLC
Chambersburg PA
CBHW081326040426
42453CB00013B/2312